Starting Off On The Right Foot

A Beginner's Guide To Running Well

by CJ Hitz

Starting Off On The Right Foot: A Beginner's Guide To Running Well

Copyright © 2012 by CJ Hitz

Body and Soul Publishing

ISBN-13: 978-0615731353
ISBN-10: 061573135X

Printed in the United States of America

Get more information here:
www.TrainWellRaceWell.com

Table of Contents

Introduction

"It's only 3.1 miles," my wife Shelley said to me. She and one of her friends decided to run a 5k race to be held less than a quarter mile from our apartment. She was now trying to persuade me to run the race.

"It's for a good cause."

Aren't they all?

So there I was, less than a mile into the race and already wishing it was over. I found myself thinking about the little things in life...like oxygen...and how it seemed to be in such short supply! I hadn't run a 5k since 1988 when I ran cross country for South Umpqua High School in Myrtle Creek, Oregon. Now I knew why...sheer pain & torture.

It was about this time that I was passed swiftly by an elderly man with a very noticeable limp in his stride and wearing a large knee brace. "Humbling" is a very accurate word to describe that moment as I watched him fade into the distance ahead of me.

27 minutes and 21 seconds after the gun fired, I finally finished in utter exhaustion, moaning and gasping in agony. As I sat down on the cold asphalt parking lot, I felt like I could die.

"Never again," I said. As far as I was concerned, that would be the last time I would sign up for that kind of misery.

That was October 21, 2006...

I would eventually run my next 5k in March of 2008 and since then, I've dropped over forty pounds in weight, chopped nearly ten minutes off my time (17:40) and competed in over 100 races ranging from 5k to 50k.

The author running the 2010 Fifth Third River Bank 5k

I can now say with 100% sincerity that I've been bitten by the ***"running bug."*** I absolutely love this most simple of sports and its many benefits.

I've devoured running magazines, books and websites looking for running tips in all categories. Some have worked while others have not.

The 5k Is A Great Place To Start

I love the 5k distance (*only* 3.1 miles). There are more 5k events held each year than all the other distances combined from the mile to the marathon. It was the distance Steve Prefontaine specialized in before his untimely death.

Simply put, the 5k is a screaming challenge that rides the line of both speed and endurance. For me, it's been a great barometer of my overall fitness and a chance to get the legs turning over faster. I actually enjoy using local 5k road races as a way to get a speed workout in and also enjoy some friendly competition.

Anyone can complete a 5k, but to see improvement, each individual has to put forth solid effort in training. As Toledo, OH running legend George Isom once told me, *"CJ, there are no miracles in running."* George was essentially saying you reap what you've sown in training.

Since I've picked up running again, I've come to appreciate numerous distances on roads and trails alike. I like to take on new challenges which helps keep me motivated to train well. By the way, one of my mottos has become, *"Train Well...Race Well."*

Achieve Your Running Goals

Whether you're sitting on the couch contemplating that first 5k or looking to get back into running after years away from the sport, I'm excited to help you achieve your goals by sharing some running & nutrition advice I've learned on my own journey. You'll also hear some helpful advice from several experienced, high-level runners with many miles under their belts.

I look forward to helping you *start off on the right foot!*

CJ Hitz

Chapter One
Wet Behind The Ears:

Tips For Beginners

First of all, before I launch into a few initial beginner tips, let me be one of the first to welcome you to the running community! Your choice to take this huge step (no pun intended) will yield many benefits in your life.

If you'll stick with it and give running a chance, you're going to eventually find yourself being 'bit by the running bug' as it's been called. The rewards you'll reap are not just physical (more energy, weight loss, etc.) but also mental, emotional and social. Every runner, no matter their level, was a beginner at some point. For me, I picked running back up in the spring of 2008 after nearly twenty years off and I can honestly say I've seen my passion for this sport increase each year.

6 tips to help get you started...

1. **Set aside 30 minutes A Day For Running** - We runners have to be intentional about including the run in our busy day. If not, we can easily fill the day with other "more important" activities. Imagine if you were scheduled to run with your boss? How likely would you be to cancel that running appointment? Get into the habit of treating every run like that. Speaking of habits, you've probably heard that it takes 21 days to form a habit. In reality, to truly make running a healthy habit, some studies reveal that it could take double that amount of time. Becoming a better runner takes

time and consistency which is one of the most important beginner tips.

2. **Walk If You Have To** - We have some friends in our local running club who like to mix in walking with running. Studies have shown this can be a positive mental lift for those getting started. If you find yourself struggling to maintain a running stride, try running for 3 minutes and then walk for 1 minute to catch your breath. As your fitness improves, you can increase your running to 4 minutes and then walk for 1 minute, increase to 5 minutes then walk 1, etc. Eventually, you'll be able to run for 30 minutes without taking any walk breaks.

3. **Find What Works For You** - Many runners run all seven days of the week. Others may run twice. Perhaps you might be able to aim for every other day. My brother-in-law has been running three days a week - two weekdays and one longer run over the weekend. Since he began, he's continued to see huge improvement in his 5k time and he just completed his first half-marathon! Ultimately, find a schedule that allows you to be consistent week in and week out. Aiming for two runs should be the minimum amount you settle for as a beginner.

4. **Join a Local Running Club** - My wife Shelley & I have met so many new friends through local running clubs we've joined. Not only does our membership give us certain benefits like discounts for races or local businesses, but we also have access to weekly group runs and running communities that give us encouragement

& motivation. Visit www.RRCA.org (Road Runners Club of America) for a listing of running clubs in your area. Of all the beginner running tips, this can help you build accountability and community to keep you going when you feel like giving up.

5. **Sign Up For A Race** - Nothing motivates me to train consistently like coughing up the cash and signing up for a race. When you put your money where your mouth is, you're now committed. As a beginner, try finding a local 5k (3.1 miles) 9 to 10 weeks away in order to gain some fitness beforehand. You won't be setting any records in this race but it's important to set a goal. What is that goal? You have to decide. It may be just finishing. It might be to run the whole distance without walking. Whatever your goal, make it something that requires a moderate level of effort to achieve but isn't unrealistic at the same time. As a beginning runner, you're trying to build confidence in the early stages. Soon enough, you'll be setting loftier goals that require greater intensity in effort to attain.

6. **Log Your Miles** - Tracking your mileage in a running log is a great way to measure your progress. There have been many times when I looked through an old log to see what I did for a certain workout or how I treated an injury. You'll find these at your local running store or online. My favorite running log is made by Nathan Sports (www.nathansports.com). If you'd rather keep track of your runs online there are a variety of logs to choose from. My favorite is www.Running2Win.com

We used to live near a local car dealership that had the following motto in many of their advertisements: *"Our goal is to make you a customer for life!"* As you begin the wonderful, simple sport of running, my hope would be for you to become a *runner for life!*

Chapter Two:
What is Nutrition?

And Why is Nutrition Important for Runners?

What is nutrition and what impact does it have on your running? And why is nutrition important for runners? Has either of these questions ever crossed your mind? Unfortunately, many runners neglect this important key to success.

Imagine If...

You could choose _any_ car you wanted, regardless of the bells & whistles offered? What would you choose? Lamborghini? Mercedes? Rolls Royce?

Oh, and one other detail...

It's the _only_ car you'll ever get for life.

Would that change your decision? After picking out the car you'll be driving for life, how would you treat it? How often would you change the oil, rotate the tires, change the brakes, have the inside detailed, wash & wax the outside?

The knowledge that we only get one of something, whether a car, a house or even a bicycle would certainly motivate us to treat those things with a little extra tender loving care.

Why Nutrition is Important: One Body For Life

So why would it be any different with our bodies? We only get one for life.

How are you treating yours?

As runners, we're breaking our bodies down with each run we complete. And that's where the importance of nutrition comes in!

What is nutrition? Nutrition is simply the provision, to our bodies, of the materials necessary (in the form of food) to support life. In other words, we have to rebuild what we break down!

Are you aware that...

- Every 6 months, 60% of our body is brand new...regenerated from scratch
- Every 7 years, 95% of our body is brand new at the cellular level
- We each have the ability to re-create our physical existence from the ground up

Some of us may be horrified to realize what kind of body we've been building over the last six months, let alone seven years. None of us would knowingly consume rat poison on a daily basis but what about poisons in the form of processed, chemically-laden foods?

In The Driver's Seat

As a runner, if you could choose <u>any</u> body, what would you choose? What materials would it be made of? What kind of energy level would it have? How about the muscle, ligament and tendon structure?

It's true that each of us has different genetics, but we shouldn't use that as an excuse for mediocrity. Each of us has the ability to reach our full God-given potential.

Unfortunately, nutrition is a stumbling block for many trying to reach that potential.

Some questions I'll try to answer include...

- What foods should I eat before a workout?
- What foods should I eat after a workout?
- When is it best to eat?
- Are all foods created equal?
- Is it true that '*You are what you eat?*'
- Is there such thing as "healing" foods?

So, what is nutrition? Well, one thing I know for sure (from experience), is that proper nutrition is crucial for the runner.

After all, you only get one body for life!

Over the next 7 chapters, we're going to take a look at some key aspects of nutrition for runners and why it's a major part of starting off on the right foot.

Elite Runner Spotlight:
Geoff Roes

Geoff Roes is one of the most accomplished ultra runners (anything longer than a marathon) in the world today. As a 2-time Ultra Runner of the Year, he's won some of the most prestigious trail ultras across North America while setting numerous course records along the way. A few of his wins include the Western States 100, Wasatch 100, American River 50, Ultra Race of Champions 100k and the Chuckanut 50k. He was also featured in the documentary *Unbreakable: The Western States 100* (www.ws100film.com)

Here's Geoff's response to the question, *"What are 3 of the most valuable things you've learned as a runner?"*

1.) Patience. It's easy to talk about being patient, both in running and in everything else in life, but it's a lot harder to actually practice patience when situations demand it. Running forces you to learn this though, as there are times when the only two choices you have are to stop altogether or keep plugging along with a deep level of patience. Sometimes we choose to stop, but those times when we choose to keep moving, we almost always learn a new appreciation for patience in our running and in our lives.

2.) I've learned to appreciate nature in a whole new way. Not as something to conquer or to use for our pleasure, but as something to immerse ourselves in and learn from its subtle cadence, beauty, and wisdom.

3.) Lastly I've learned the importance of friendship and community. I've been on hundreds of amazing runs on my own, but it's the sharing of this passion with others that has given me the most joy. Seeing other people excited for life through the lens of running out in the mountains is probably the most inspiring thing I've ever known.

To follow Geoff and his running adventures, visit his blog "Fumbling Toward Endurance"...
www.akrunning.blogspot.com

Geoff also organizes an ultrarunning camp in Alaska each summer...
www.akultracamp.blogspot.com

Chapter Three:
Runner Nutrition

What Should I Eat *Before* I Run?

Optimal athlete nutrition is vital for runners. It's especially important to put the right "fuel" into your body before and after a run.

Thus, the question, *"What should I eat before I run?"*

When I was going to college in Anderson, Indiana there was a gas station close to campus where my friends and I would fill up our cars. Not only was this a convenient location, it also had the cheapest gas...*in more ways than one*. This station gained a reputation for having 'watered down' gasoline. No wonder our fuel mileage was suffering, not to mention any possible damage to the engine!

When it comes to *runner nutrition* and powering the human body, there are quality sources of fuel and 'watered down' sources of fuel.

From an athlete nutrition standpoint, not all foods are created equal. Gaining some knowledge in this area can mean the difference between feeling full of energy or feeling sluggish and faint as you run-otherwise known as bonking. I've experienced both and I'll take 'full of energy' any day!

Nutrition Tip #1: Fuel Systems 101

For the runner, carbohydrates are the fuel of choice due to the quickness in which the body can break them down. The most common carb is glucose.

Glucose is like a matchstick that helps you burn fat as well as the only fuel our brains use. It's also what powers our central nervous system.

Where's glucose found naturally? Fruits & honey are the most nutrient dense sources of calories. And it's because of that nutrient density that natural is always better than the man-made, genetically-altered, chemically-loaded substitutes that leave our bodies feeling cheated.

Pound for pound, fruit is the best source of carb energy. Some delicious examples include...

- Bananas

- Dates
- Oranges
- Pineapple
- Grapes
- Apples
- Strawberries
- Blueberries
- Melon

Not only do these fruits provide the glucose our bodies crave, but they're also great sources of fiber that help bind up the waste that our bodies produce.

Studies have shown that most Americans consume an average of 5g of fiber in their diet each day. We're supposed to get 50g. When you consider that a small dish of blueberries provides 15g, it doesn't seem like it should be so difficult to reach that 50g.

Nutrition Tip #2: Refined = Robbed

Foods that have been refined and processed have been robbed of critical nutrients found only in natural, whole food sources. For example, high fructose corn syrup has been isolated from its whole food source (corn) and placed in countless products that make their way onto our local grocery store shelves (crackers, cookies, soft drinks, sport drinks to name a few).

White bread is another example of a food where valuable nutrients have been refined or taken out. Bread made from whole grains is less refined and retains more nutrient value, thus providing a runner's body more of what it truly craves. You may pay less for that loaf of white bread, but you're still being robbed in the end.

As you might imagine, not all calories are created equal. Some are nutrient dense (fruit, whole grains, veggies) and some are just plain empty (or should I say "wimpy").

A few examples of foods full of empty calories include...

- Soft drinks
- Candy bars
- Chips
- Several varieties of snack crackers and cookies
- Many breakfast cereals
- Fruit "drinks" (as opposed to real juice)

Now I'll certainly admit to enjoying a candy bar as a sweet treat from time to time, but not to fuel my training runs or races.

When we indulge on foods full of empty calories, it's easy to over consume due to their lack of nutrient content. At this point, the body shuts down (that low you feel after the quick high) in order to compensate for the sugar overload. The last thing you want as a runner is a quick high and then...crash! Game over baby.

Therefore, it's very important to look at the ingredients listed on any item that may catch your interest. There are many products promoting themselves as "healthy" athlete nutrition that are anything but. For example, many diet or protein bars are full of refined sugars and high fructose corn syrup. Don't settle for that junk, it's simply a waste of your money.

Nutrition Tip #3: *When* Should I Eat Before I Run?

An <u>optimal</u> time to consume your fuel for a training run would be 2 1/2 to 3 hours beforehand, but it really depends on the distance you plan on going. I used the word "optimal" in that first sentence because the body has had adequate time to fully digest and absorb the fuel. In other words, it's available for use. Eating too much without the proper digestion time will many times lead to a side stitch or pain in your side.

Technically, our bodies have enough carb stores to get us through a 5-8 mile run in the morning without any problem, depending on your pace. But it's wise to consume something beforehand, especially if you feel low on energy after waking up.

Different foods may vary in digestion time. A banana, for example, will digest faster than a piece of whole grain toast. Both are good carb sources but the banana is better when you have less time before your run.

One of my favorite fuel choices is a fruit smoothie for the ease of digestion. Food in liquid form gets into the bloodstream more rapidly. Solid food has to be broken down in the stomach before becoming available.

Nutrition Tip #4: Pre-Run Smoothie

Let me close by sharing one of my favorite pre-run smoothies...

- 10 ounces purified water
- 1 banana
- 5 strawberries
- ½ cup blueberries
- 2 medjool dates
- Ice for texture
- 2-3oz apple juice for added sweetener (optional)
- Blend until smooth

Total nutrient dense calories = 200

- When possible, I always buy organic, especially with fruits where I eat the skin
- The above ingredients are also outstanding when frozen
- Pre-run smoothies can be consumed 1 ½ - 2 hrs before a run since they digest faster

I discuss the value of smoothies more in-depth in my book *Smoothies For Runners* where I also share 32 delicious recipes (www.SmoothiesForRunners.com)

Chapter Four:
Post Workout Nutrition

What Should I Eat *After* I Run?
The Importance of Recovery for Runners

Early on, I found that my post workout nutrition - what I put into my body after a run - is one of the most important parts of my training. Why is nutrition for recovery so important? Let me show you!

Hungry?

So you've just returned from an intense hour long training run that has you feeling famished. You're hungry so you just grab the first thing in sight right?

Wrong!

Post workout nutrition after a hard workout or race is just as important as the workout itself. What have you done in the previous hour?

You've broken down your body through vigorous exercise. Even during the workout there's a point where the body begins scrambling for rebuilding materials to help repair muscles, tendons, ligaments and bones.

Haiti: An Observation

On January 12, 2010 the world was shocked upon hearing the news of a devastating 7.0 earthquake that killed over 300,000 people and left over a million homeless. My wife Shelley had the opportunity to serve on a medical team nearly a month afterward and she was at a loss for words regarding the damage & devastation around Port Au Prince. Architectural experts have said the loss of life could have been much less if Haiti had stricter building codes in place.

A little over a month later, Chile experienced a much more powerful earthquake measuring 8.8 on the Richter Scale yet the total deaths numbered 521. It's no coincidence that Chile's building codes are much stricter than those in Haiti.

One question remains...

How will Haiti rebuild?

That's also an important question for the runner. In other words, what materials will we give the body to work with in our post workout nutrition?

The body goes into rebuilding mode immediately. The window of time after a workout to guarantee maximum repair is 15 minutes. It's the most important 15 minutes of your entire workout. It's the time that you ensure nutrition recovery from today's run and, in the process, prepare yourself for tomorrow's run.

It really can make or break your success...or your body!

An Ingredient For Success

An important part of post workout nutrition is to replace glycogen stores in the muscles that we lose during the run. Glycogen is what fuels our bodies to function, whether running or just thinking with our brains. The two main sources of glycogen storage in our bodies are the liver and muscles. Our liver can store about 80g which is enough for about 18 minutes of exercise. Our muscles can store 350g which is enough for 70 minutes of exercise.

The "wall" people refer to in a marathon is the point at which those folks have used up stored glycogen.

For an elite marathoner, this is around mile 20. For the average runner, this may be in miles 16-18. Whether you're elite or average, when the body uses up the glycogen stores, it's finished. Draining glycogen stores isn't as much of a concern for races or training runs of 10 miles or less. But it's still important to replace what you use during those efforts.

Re-Fueling Suggestions

As we've mentioned before, our bodies are in a constant state of regeneration right down to the cellular level. This process only speeds up for the runner since we're breaking down our bodies and rebuilding on a daily basis.

This is why it's crucial that we refrain from refueling our bodies with artificial, chemically laden food substitutes that our bodies can't process & use. Do you really want your body to be one big molecular candy bar or bag of chips? Whole foods are what the body is craving in the nutrition recovery stage.

Here are some of my favorite foods for post workout nutrition...

Clif Bars & Larabars - made of organic ingredients, these little guys are ideal when you're short on time. They range from 200-260 calories each depending on flavor and there's a nice balance of carbohydrate (fuel) &

protein (rebuilding material). You'll find them in most grocery stores.

Greek Yogurt with Berries - Greek yogurt is packed with protein that our bodies use to rebuild tissues broken down in the run. The berries are full of powerful antioxidants that go after those free radical cells produced from activity. Dark colored berries have also been shown to help decrease inflammation caused during strenuous exercise. Consider them nature's anti-inflammatory!

Examples include blueberries, strawberries, grapes, blackberries, cranberries and cherries.

Fruit & Protein Smoothie - This is by far my favorite way to refuel. Why? Ease of digestion and availability for the body. By blending various ingredients together into liquid form, the body can immediately send the nutrients where they need to go rather than breaking down solid food first. Anytime I get a smoothie into my body within that 15 minute window, I feel less soreness, stiffness and general fatigue, even after an intense workout.

Here's one of my favorite nutrition recovery smoothies...

- 8oz Rice Dream brand rice milk
- 4oz Bolthouse Farms "Berry Boost" flavor drink - made from pure fruit
- Handful of organic spinach leaves
- 1 scoop *Vega Sport* Vanilla protein powder (vegan friendly)
- 1/2 cup frozen wild blueberries
- 1/2 frozen banana
- 2 tbsp ground flax seed (provides omega 3 & 6 essential fatty acids)

- Blend until smooth (I use a Vita-Mix Super 5000...well worth the investment!)

Total Calories = 480; Total Protein = 24g; Total Fat = 10.5g

For more on my philosophy of protein powders, please visit this page – www.smoothiesforrunners.com/protein-powder

Chapter Five
Runners Diet:

Are Fruits & Vegetables Part of Yours?

As a runner, what kind of diet do you have? In talking with runners of all levels from casual jogger to elite marathoner, I've noticed one food group in particular that seems to be deficient in their diet: The fruit & veggie group. We runners tend to go heavy in the breads, grains, pastas and meat category thinking that will be our quickest route to carbohydrate & protein replenishment. We'll scarf down a banana or some carrots but we seldom get much more adventurous. In the process, our bodies are truly missing out on some fantastic runner nutrition.

Fruit & Vegetable Nutrition Facts

We've known for some time that most Americans don't come anywhere close to eating the 7-13 servings of fruit & veggies every day, as recommended by the USDA. But the situation is worse than we thought.

A new report issued by the U.S. Centers for Disease Control (CDC) reveals that more than two-thirds of adults eat fruit fewer than twice a day, and almost three-quarters eat vegetables fewer than 3 times daily. Even more disheartening, another report issued by the CDC found that less than 10% of high school students manage to eat 5 servings or more of fruit and veggies daily.

Numerous studies have highlighted the connection between eating fruit & vegetables and decreased risk of a host of chronic diseases, such as heart disease, stroke, cancer, and diabetes. A lack of fruit & veggies is also correlated with an increased risk of obesity. That's relevant, when we consider that a team of researchers at Harvard University just predicted that the obesity rate in the United States will keep rising until it reaches 42% (currently 34%).

"Healthy People 2010" Falls Short

The last time the CDC conducted a survey of eating habits of American adults was in 2000. Disturbed by the extremely low level of fruit and vegetable consumption at that time, the U.S. government launched Healthy People 2010 – a set of health objectives for the nation to achieve over the first decade of the new century.

The goals of Healthy People 2010 were modest. The project aimed to get 75% of Americans to eat at least 2 servings of fruit per day, and 50% to eat at least 3 servings of vegetables. Even though the government has made efforts to encourage people to eat better, the new CDC report found absolutely no change in vegetable consumption compared to ten years ago, and a slight decrease in fruit consumption.

The CDC's report isn't the only one to expose the woeful lack of fruit and vegetables in American diets. In 2007, researchers from the Johns Hopkins School of Public Health and the Welch Center for Prevention, Epidemiology, and Clinical Research determined that 72% of Americans did not meet even the minimal guidelines for fruit consumption (2 servings); and 68% did not meet the minimal guidelines for veggie consumption (3 servings). All told, fewer than 11% met Healthy People 2010's modest goal of 5 total servings per day.

Clearly, people in the United States are not consuming enough fruit and vegetables. But how much are they actually eating? According to the USDA, not much. While the Dietary Guidelines recommend eating 7-13 servings, Americans report eating just 4.4 servings.

Keep in mind – that's how much they report eating. Research has found that people typically overestimate the amount of fruit and veggies they eat, and underestimate the amount of fats and sweets. Also keep in mind that people include less healthy "vegetable" choices, such as french fries, in these figures.

A Runners Diet = A Higher Standard

We runners cannot afford to "just get by" when it comes to fruit & veggies. Each time we enjoy a workout, we not only burn calories but we also create oxidation throughout our bodies. And the byproduct of oxidation is what we call free radicals. These are the unruly cells that cause disease. We've all seen the effects of rust on metal which is also caused by oxidation. Oxidation speeds up the aging process in all of us.

In recent years, the term "anti-oxidants" has been quite a buzz word in nutrition circles. Thousands of new supplements claiming to be full of powerful anti-oxidants are hitting our shelves each year. Here's a little hint...

Walk right past those "gimmick" shelves and head straight for the produce aisle!

Only in buying the whole fruit and vegetable will you get the most nutritious effect. Each fruit & veggie contains literally thousands of nutrients including valuable anti-oxidants that work together as a team.

The supplement companies have isolated individual nutrients and bottled them up to sell by the truck load. Studies have shown this to actually be dangerous for our bodies.

Imagine a football coach leaving his quarterback on the field but removing the other ten players he needs in order to win. You don't need to be an ESPN announcer to know what would happen. A football team is 11 players each carrying out their assignments side by side. Think of that apple as a team of vitamins, minerals and anti-oxidants each carrying out their assignments in the body side by side.

The fact is popping pills has become the cheap substitute to eating real fruit & veggies in this country. If we intend to maximize our potential as runners, we simply cannot settle for these cheap substitutes. The runners' diet has to set the standard.

Have you given your body some fruit & veggie lovin' lately?

Let me close by sharing one of my favorite veggie salads that's sure to help you reach those 7-13 servings of fruit & veggies we need daily...

- Medium sized bowl (bigger than your cereal bowls!)
- Fill ¾ of the bowl with mixed salad greens
- 1/4 green or red bell pepper sliced into small pieces
- 6 baby carrots sliced into small pieces
- 6 cherry tomatoes each sliced in half
- 6 sugar snap peas sliced into pieces
- 6 slices zucchini
- 6 slices cucumber

- 6 broccoli florets
- 6 green or black olives
- Small handful Alfalfa sprouts
- 12 raw or salted almonds
- Light amount of crumbled feta cheese sprinkled on top (optional)
- 3 TBSP Newman's Own brand low fat Asian dressing
- Mix together & enjoy the veggie goodness!

*When possible I always buy organic, especially with produce where the outside peel is eaten.

Chapter Six
12 Fantastic Foods That Yield High Nutrition for Runners

When it comes to our diets, we runners need food that packs a punch in the nutrition category. Settling for anything less is robbing our bodies of the fuel and rebuilding blocks that keep us injury free day in and day out. If the phrase "*You are what you eat*" is true, we runners live that out on a daily basis since we're breaking down our bodies and rebuilding with each glorious run.

The following 12 foods should be part of every runner's diet in one way, shape or form. These foods provide the nutrients necessary to run faster, recover quicker, and feel full of energy all day long. They also contain disease-fighting qualities according to study after study.

#1: Almonds

These little guys can satisfy those cravings that we runners experience throughout the day. Each serving (about 22 almonds) provides 6g protein, 14g of healthy monounsaturated fat, and 170 calories. Packed with vitamin E, almonds can help heal muscle damage and ward off age-related diseases. One of my favorite snacks anytime of the day.

#2: Apples

I'm sure you've heard the phrase "*An apple a day keeps the doctor away.*" It's a true statement through and through. At the "core" of this catchy adage, apples really will help prolong the time between doctor visits. One medium sized apple (3" in diameter) contains 4g of dietary fiber which is 8% of what our bodies need daily! 25g of carbs and 95 calories will aid in fueling a run. Apples contain a significant amount of the flavonoid Quercetin which helps boost immunity in resisting cold & flu bugs. If possible, buy organic and eat the skin in order to get the maximum amount of nutrients.

#3: Bananas

This potassium-packed fruit may be the most popular among runners. It seems there is no shortage of bananas waiting for runners on refreshment tables at races of all distances. With 27g of carbs and a healthy dose of vitamin B-6, these yellow wonders aren't just for monkeys. Eat a banana or two before your next race of 10 miles or longer in order to help stave off cramps (thanks to the potassium).

#4: Broccoli

Few foods can stand up to this flowered friend when it comes to overall nutrition. In the vegetable world, green = goodness. Sulforaphane, a phytochemical found in broccoli, has been found to selectively kill cancer cells. As if this is not enough, this cruciferous veggie is high in vitamin C, folate, calcium, and vitamin K (bone-building). Eat up!

#5: Brown Rice

Whether you're using it with stir fry, soups, or breakfast (flavor with cinnamon, honey, raisins) brown rice is a carbohydrate heavy-weight with over 45g per 1 cup serving. You're also sure to get plenty of healthy antioxidants with every bite.

#6: Black Beans

Considered a "meat" of vegetarians, this legume is certainly legit. A runner's diet is only enhanced when adding the "magical fruit" to the mix. Each 1 cup serving will give you 225 calories, 41g of carbs, 15g of protein, and a whopping 15g (30% of daily need) of dietary fiber! Use in soups, dips, or throw on top of your steamed brown rice.

#7: Flax Seed

Add a tablespoon of ground flax seed to your smoothies or salads and you'll be adding a great source of alpha-linolenic acid - a good fat that helps boost immunity, blood flow, and prevents blood clots. Flax has also been known to possibly increase endurance. 60 calories you can afford to consume!

#8: Chocolate

No, that's not a typo! 1oz of this pure bliss contains 17g of carbs and 160 calories. The healthiest (in moderation of course) chocolate should contain at least 60% cacao. The higher the cacao concentration, the bitterer it will be. Partaking of this treat will give you the same phytochemicals found in red wine that are known to fight heart disease by keeping the artery walls clean. Go ahead, eat without guilt!

#9: Oatmeal

You certainly can't go wrong by eating this cholesterol lowering food. A ½ cup serving will give you 150 calories, 27g of carbs, 5.5g of protein, and a healthy dose of iron. Add dried cherries and slivered almonds for a flavorful breakfast. Eating oatmeal before any long run or race of over 10 miles has become my favorite pre-race routine as it provides slow-release carbs to the bloodstream. I always feel more than sustained in terms of energy.

#10: Salmon

A 3oz serving of this tasty fish will give you a hefty 22g of tissue-building protein, 4g of good fat, and only 130 calories, giving you quite a bang for the buck. Salmon is an incredible source of omega-3 fatty acids which helps guard against heart disease. It's also a great source of vitamin B-12 which aids in brain function. When shopping for salmon, <u>always</u> look for wild caught salmon and stay away from farm raised. I'm partial to the wild Alaskan variety myself.

#11: Spinach

Again, green = goodness. If it's good enough for Popeye, it's good enough for us runners. Just a ½ cup serving provides a nice dose of calcium and iron. Spinach is also high in carotenes which help stave off age-related diseases. One study found that 1-3 servings of raw spinach each week can virtually eliminate macular degeneration (the macula is part of the retina in the eye) in elderly patients. Keep it raw baby! Add to smoothies or make a spinach salad by adding walnuts, crumbled bleu cheese, dried cherries and low-fat raspberry vinaigrette.

#12: Blueberries

One of my favorite times of the year is blueberry season. Blueberries are one of nature's anti-inflammatories, which means they're a runner's friend. No need for ibuprofen when you have access to blueberries. These little blue power pellets contain high amounts of antioxidants which aid in blood flow and also provide a nice bit of dietary fiber. Add fresh or frozen berries to that post-run smoothie to help decrease inflammation which causes soreness. You can also add blueberries to your breakfast cereal or whole-grain pancakes & waffles.

Begin working these 12 fantastic foods into your diet and your body will thank you.

Elite Runner Spotlight: Peter Maksimow

Peter Maksimow is one of the premier Mountain/Trail runners in the United States today, though he's not opposed to running a fast road race from time to time. Some of Peter's running accomplishments include...

*2005 - Member of the US Mountain Running Team
*3-time member of the US Mountain Running Team Champions (2005, 2010, 2012)
*2-time Colorado State 50K Champion (2011, 2012)
*USATF Colorado State 25K Champion (2012)
*4-time Top 10 finisher Pikes Peak Ascent (2003, 2010, 2011, 2012)
*Incline Beer Mile Champion 25:45 (2012) – For more on the infamous Incline of Manitou Springs, CO visit www.cospringstrails.com/hikes/incline.html

Here's Peter's response to the question, *"What are 3 of the most valuable things you've learned as a runner?"*

1.) One of the most valuable things I've learned as a runner is that you can't pretend when it comes to fitness. You can't miraculously lay down an amazing race if you haven't put in the work. If you haven't put in the time and training, it will rear its ugly head in a race. No pretending there. People sometimes say to me "I wish I could run as fast as you." There is no trick, other than having a bit of natural ability and seeing how far you can push that ability with good old fashioned 'hard work'. The training will dictate the results.

2.) Training is a cumulative effect. The results are rarely

seen in a month or a year, but rather in a number of years or decades.

3.) Running has taught me to appreciate nature. Where else are you able to get out into remote areas and see nature and wildlife that very few are privileged to see?

You can keep up with Peter's running at Team Colorado's Blog...

www.TeamColorado.blogspot.com

Photo Credit: Tim Bergsten

Chapter Seven:
Running to Lose Weight

Some of you may have taken up running to help lose weight. Running can be a great way to help shed those excess pounds (I'm living proof). Think of running as the igniter of the flame that starts your calorie-burning furnace. That furnace is your metabolism. The more activity (running) we incorporate into our lives, the greater the body's need to burn calories to both sustain life and rebuild what's been broken down.

People go wrong in their weight loss attempts when they try to lose pounds too quickly. Slow and steady is the healthy way to lose weight. It's important to realize there are no shortcuts to losing weight - even when using running for weight loss. Slashing too many calories from our diet too quickly will leave us feeling low on energy, rob us of essential nutrients, and make us susceptible to injury.

Healthy weight loss means losing no more than 1-2 pounds a week when running to lose weight. Diet pill companies with slogans like "Lose 10 pounds in 10 days!" should be avoided at all costs. People who buy into these gimmicks and fads almost always gain the weight back...and then some.

Here are a few things to consider for runners who want to lose weight...

Don't Sacrifice Healthy Nutrition

What you eat is just as important as *how much* you eat. Increasing the amount of fruit & vegetables and decreasing the amount of empty calorie foods (i.e. soda, candy, chips) in your diet will allow you to get into a lean body mentality. Empty calories are stored as fat that will slow you down in your next race.

Perhaps you've developed a habit of eating that *Snickers* in the afternoon. After all, "*Snickers satisfies*", right? Not exactly. In a regular 2oz bar you get:

- 271 calories
- 14g of fat (5g are the dreaded saturated fat)
- 35g of carbs
- 1g of dietary fiber
- 29g of sugars (refined & high fructose corn syrup)
- 4g of protein

A healthy alternative to that candy bar could be a banana and a serving of almonds (22 almonds). Let's see how they compare as a combination:

- 265 calories (banana-105, almonds-160)
- 14g of good fat (banana-0g, almonds-14g)
- 33g carbs (banana-27g, almonds-6g)
- 6g of dietary fiber (banana-3g, almonds-3g)
- 15g of natural sugars (banana-14g, almonds-1g)
- 6g of protein (banana-0g, almonds-6g)

By making this tweak in your afternoon snack choice, you're trading empty calories for nutrient dense calories. Over the course of several weeks, you'll notice a distinct difference in your energy levels as you give your body what it truly craves. You'll also be encouraging a lean body mentality in the process of running to lose weight.

You'll Need to Burn Calories!

In order to lose one pound, you'll need to burn 3500 calories. Keep in mind you don't need to burn that many calories in one day. The average runner will burn approximately 100 calories for each mile they run when running to lose weight. It's also good to remember that we all burn a certain amount of calories each day through basic life functions (sleeping, walking, climbing stairs, house & yard work, etc). Whether it's exercise or making changes to our diet, we need to find a way to trim 3500 calories over the course of a week in order to lose that pound.

Write It Down

When I was more concerned about trimming extra pounds the method I found most helpful in monitoring calorie intake was simply writing it down. This can be done with a journal, notebook or those little yellow sticky notes which I use for many things. I keep the sticky note on my kitchen counter and write down the food and number of calories based on the serving size I ate. Besides looking at the nutrition facts on the back of the food package, another helpful resource is www.nutritiondata.com where you can find almost every food available whether packaged or whole foods (fruit, vegetables, grains).

Though it may seem like a burden to keep track of your calorie intake at first, over the course of several days, you'll gain a new sense of freedom as you regain control of what goes into your mouth daily. Healthy disciplines put us in the driver's seat rather than constantly being held hostage and jerked around by our appetites.

Let's look at an example of what a day of monitoring calories might look like:

- bowl of cereal with rice milk, blueberries - 500 cal

- cup of coffee with ½ tsp. raw sugar, 1 Tbsp. half & half - 75 cal
- fruit & protein smoothie - 500 cal
- banana & serving of almonds - 265 cal
- cup of coffee with ½ tsp. raw sugar, 1 Tbsp. half & half - 75 cal
- salmon burger with whole wheat thin buns, hummus, sprouts & veggies - 300 cal
- apple - 95 cal
- Total: 1810 calories

It's really that simple. If you really want to be detailed, you can include the time of day you ate each item (I don't do this). After a while, you get pretty good at knowing how many calories are in the foods you eat based on servings and no longer need to look them up before writing them down.

Set a Goal

It's helpful to know (as close as you're able) your ideal body weight. Initially, this may be your goal weight. For example, if you're currently 217 lbs. and want to get down to 192 lbs., your goal is to lose 25 lbs. As a 192 lb. male, you'll need to take in approximately 1900 calories each day in order to maintain this weight. If you were to run 4 miles that day, you'd need to take in an extra 400 calories to compensate for those you burned on that run. This would take you up to 2300 calories for the day in order to simply maintain that weight. Based on the 1-2 pounds a week that we mentioned above, it's going to take no less than 12 weeks for this person to reach their goal weight in a healthy way.

So as a person who weighs 217 lbs., you have to begin thinking as a 192 lb. person in order to get there. It won't happen overnight, but over the course of several weeks, you'll see yourself shedding excess pounds in a healthy manner. Thinking you'll get there quicker by just cutting out whole meals while increasing exercise isn't the smart method as we mentioned earlier.

By monitoring your caloric intake, you'll be able to cut the empty calories hindering you from reaching your goal weight. By logging your running miles, you'll be able to know how many calories you're burning each day and what you can afford to eat. It's essentially like sitting down and forming a budget in order to monitor how your money is being spent and what you can afford without going into debt.

Running for weight loss is an ideal method of exercise to help you achieve your goal of being a lean & mean machine!

A great resource on the subject of weight loss for runners is *Racing Weight* by Matt Fitzgerald. You'll find it on Amazon.com.

Chapter Eight:
Dehydration

Don't Underestimate It

As a runner it's important to consider the impact dehydration can have and to make sure you're getting enough fluids. Let me illustrate...

On one of my weekly 6 mile tempo runs with a group of friends, I began experiencing some slight cramp-like symptoms in my right hamstring. Thinking it would eventually loosen up, I continued to push the pace until it began getting worse. I told one of my running buddies I would need to back off the remainder of the run. I knew exactly what was happening...

Welcome to the land of dehydration!

To be honest, my dehydration that day (and any day) was due to pure carelessness. I drank a little more coffee that day than usual and failed to take in the amount of water my body needed. Though some studies have found coffee & soda to be nearly equal to water in terms of keeping the body hydrated, I don't buy it. My body just doesn't feel the same or perform at the same level on those high coffee/low water days. In the end, water is just cleaner and what our bodies crave the most.

Why is Hydration for the Runner So Important?

Water makes up about 60% of our body weight. When we run, we naturally lose water which leads to stiffening muscles, tendons, ligaments and joints. A running cramp is one of the ways our bodies let us know we're suffering from dehydration. I found this out the hard way at the 18 mile mark of the 2008 Akron Marathon. Both hamstrings began cramping and forced me to stop for ten minutes. A police officer noticed the difficulty I was having and actually offered me a bottle of water from his squad car! I gladly accepted. Unfortunately, it's almost impossible to reverse the effects of dehydration in a training run or race. This is why we need to stay hydrated throughout the day rather than trying to cram it all in at the last moment.

Here are some important benefits of water and body function:

- Regulates body temperature
- Moistens tissues for mouth, eyes and nose
- Lubricates joints (like oil in a car engine)
- Protects organs and tissues
- Helps prevent constipation
- Reduces the burden on kidneys & liver by flushing waste products

- Helps dissolve minerals & other nutrients to make available for the body
- Carries nutrients & oxygen to cells

A few Signs of Mild Dehydration:

- Lack of saliva
- Decreased output of urine
- Deep color and strong odor in urine
- Thirst - simply being thirsty is a sign we haven't been drinking enough

How Much Water Do I Need?

We runners will naturally need more water than those who aren't as active. On a day off, I use the following formula for my water consumption:

Body weight divided by 2, then change this number to ounces. For example, my body weight is 160 lbs. Dividing this by 2 = 80 lbs. Therefore, I need at least 80oz of water each day. This number increases when we run in order to replace what we lose in sweat.

When the weather is warmer, our bodies will require even more water due to evaporation. Depending on body weight, each person will vary in sweat loss rate. To find out your personal sweat loss rate, weigh yourself in the nude before going out on a timed training run. Weigh yourself again in the nude upon your return. One pound of weight loss = one pint of water loss. For example, if you lose 2 lbs. of weight in a one hour run, you've lost 2 pints (32oz) of water. This same person would lose 16oz of water on a 30 minute run.

**Note: Studies have found that as little as 2% dehydration can have a negative effect on a race performance.

If I'm going out for a one hour run, I like to drink at least 20oz or more of water 30-45 minutes before my run. This allows enough time for the water to empty the stomach and get where it needs to throughout the body. None of us like that "sloshy" water feeling in the stomach. Drinking too much or eating too close to a run can also lead to those pesky side stitches that seem to take forever to go away.

When I first began running, I carried a water bottle on any run over 30 minutes. After experimenting with my water needs since then, I've realized I don't need to take in fluid during runs that are under 90 minutes, unless it's a very warm day. On a long run day (over 90 minutes), I either carry a water bottle or run a route where I have access to a drinking fountain. A rule of thumb is to experiment on your training runs so you know how your body will react on race day. You don't want to find yourself dehydrated on your long run and still a long way from home. No fun.

Is it Possible to Over-Hydrate?

Absolutely. Over-hydrating can lead to hyponatremia, a dangerous condition caused by drinking too much fluid. Quite simply, hyponatremia happens when the sodium level in the body becomes diluted (literally flooding the body). In the most serious cases, brain swelling that could lead to seizures and other life-threatening complications can occur. Talk about being watered down! This is one reason it's a good idea to take in some form of electrolyte sports drink on those long runs. By doing so, you replace some of the sodium lost. If I'm going to hydrate with a sports drink, I prefer HEED (www.hammernutrition.com) or Nuun tablets (www.nuun.com) since they're made with healthier ingredients.

Dial in the proper hydration for your body and your running is sure to start off on the right foot.

Elite Runner Spotlight:
Brandy Erholtz

Brandy Erholtz has a reputation for being one of the top trail/mountain runners throughout the United States and abroad. Though she especially excels in races that have significant climbing involved, Brandy has also enjoyed plenty of success in flat road and trail races as well as winter snowshoe races. Brandy possesses an enthusiasm that's contagious and continues to serve as an inspiration and mentor to the young runners she coaches.

Highlights:
*5x Member of U.S. Mountain Running Team (2008-2012)
*Team Gold World Mountain Running Championships (2012)
*2008 & 2009 Mt. Washington Road Race winner
*2008 & 2009 U.S. Mountain Runner of the Year
*2009 & 2010 Barr Trail Race Winner & Course Record Holder
*2009 & 2011 U.S. National Snowshoe Champion
*2009 & 2010 Teva Mountain Games 10K Champion
*2012 Colfax 10 Miler Champion Overall (male & female)
*2009 4th Bolder Boulder
*2008 9th U.S. 10 Mile National Championships
*2007 Tucson Marathon Champion

Here's Brandy's response to the question, *"What are 3 of the most valuable things you've learned as a runner?"*

1.) Don't set limits on what you can achieve! Dream big and set goals, with health, hard work and perseverance anything is possible.

2.) Don't take yourself so seriously. Running is a gift, in the end, it doesn't matter if you won or lost the most races or even what your personal records are. It truly is the experiences and people you meet along the way that truly matter. In the end, a race is a just a race! Have fun and take in the scenery!

3.) Surround yourself with positive people who encourage you and support your goals. If you have faith, pray.

A couple of Brandy's favorite verses are...

"I can do all things through Christ who gives me strength." (Philippians 4:13)

"Be strong and courageous." (Deuteronomy 31:6)

One other quote Brandy has always liked is, *"Temporary setbacks are opportunities in disguise."*

Photo Credit: Keith Ladzinski

Chapter Nine:
When Is It Time For New Running Shoes?

If you're like me, you like to get the most out of the things you buy. In the case of cars, my wife and I like to drive them until they die. We had a 1990 Geo Prizm we put nearly 200,000 miles on before giving it to a friend who was in need. Our 2006 Chevy Aveo recently passed the 170,000 mile mark...just breaking it in, right? When it comes to clothing, my wife gives me a hard time when we begin seeing holes from all the wear. Unfortunately, when it comes to running shoes, I had to learn the hard way.

Running Shoes: A Different Animal

There are lots of things in life we can wear out completely and feel no adverse effects. Our running shoes are not one of those things. All running shoes come with a certain amount of cushioning...some more, some less. Running shoes also have a certain level of tread on the bottom...some more, some less. Some shoes are made specifically for heavier runners and some are geared toward Kenyans...I mean lighter runners. Typically, a more cushioned shoe is going to give us more mileage than the leaner, minimal shoes.

When a running shoe begins to wear out, our bodies have a tendency to let us know. This is how I've had to learn the hard way. I've had many pairs of running shoes that I tried to "squeeze out" more miles than the previous pair, only to end up feeling little nagging aches in my legs. When it's time for new running shoes, I tend to notice the aches in my knees and quads.

The knee pain shows up due to the foot strike being compromised as the shoe wears down. The quad pain occurs due to the lack of cushioning and shock absorption. Have you ever experienced your quads aching a little more than usual after a long run on the roads? Some of this may be natural but some could be attributed to the pounding the legs are taking with worn out running shoes. Shin splints are also a common indicator that it's time for new running shoes.

These nagging little aches can turn into nagging "little" running injuries if we continue to gamble with worn out running shoes. As a runner, everything begins with our feet. They are the foundation that the weight of our body relies upon. Think of a firm foundation that a house needs in order to stand. Any architect will tell you that when a foundation begins to deteriorate, the house is on shaky ground.

A Few Signs It May Be Time For New Running Shoes

1. **Unusual aches & pains** - particularly in the knees, quads or shins - some shin splints are a direct result of worn out shoes
2. **Sole tread** - the bottom of the shoe has worn smooth in one or more places
3. **High Mileage** - Once your running shoes have over 400 miles on them, it's time to begin thinking about new shoes. Some pairs may last well over 500 miles but not all shoes are created equal.
4. **Twist Test** - New shoes are stiffer until they are gradually broken in. If you can twist your running shoes like a pair of slippers, it may be time for a new pair.
5. **Table Test** - If your shoes lean significantly (due to wear) in a certain direction when you lay them on a table, time to head to the running store

A Few Helpful Running Shoe Tips

1. **Rotating Shoes** - When you find a pair you like (and your feet like), buy a couple pairs if funds allow. It's wise to have two pairs you can rotate back and forth and allows more time before the need to shop again. I've gone with the Nike Lunarfly for the last 9-10 pairs of trainers I've bought. My feet love them and they're a good fit. For you, it may be another brand or model.
2. **Keep track in your running log** - Once you mark the day you bought the shoes, it's easy to go back and add up the mileage you've run in them.
3. **Wear your running shoes for running only** - This will save on unnecessary wear and add to the shoe lifespan.

4. **Refrain from the washing machine** - I admit, I've been guilty in this category. Instead, use a scrub brush, mild soap and cold water if the shoes need cleaned. Allow to air dry afterward.

Knowing when it's time for new running shoes is like knowing when to change the tires on your car. Waiting too long can be a potential disaster for both your car and your body. Show your feet some love and they'll take you where you want to go...without the extra aches and pains along the way.

CJ's Lessons Learned...
Shoe Selection and the
'Agony of De Feet'

For as long as I can remember, I've always loved getting new shoes. Whether it was a new pair of basketball high tops or a pair of football cleats, I loved the process of shopping for shoes growing up. The older I get, the more I like finding great deals on shoes!

For the runner, shoes are perhaps the most important piece of equipment we buy. If you're like me, once you find a pair of running shoes that fit and perform well, you keep coming back to them again and again.

Recently, I bought a pair of Nike XC Waffle Racers that weigh less than 5 ounces each. I had worn them for only a couple training runs before deciding to wear them for the Lead King Loop 25k trail race in Marble, CO. The race begins with ½ mile of flat dirt road before climbing 2900 ft. over the next 5 miles. Once at the top of the climb, runners begin a brutal 10 mile descent on rough jeep road filled with scree, bowling ball-sized rocks and tough footing en route to the finish.

The shoes felt great on the climb to the top. In fact, the only real experimenting I'd done in them was primarily uphill. Unfortunately, I learned one of the most painful lessons in my running career on that mean descent. I began feeling some blisters forming at around the 8 mile mark. This is a dreadful feeling when you still have over 7 miles of rough terrain ahead of you.

By the 10 mile mark, my feet were in shear agony. These shoes were made for tame, soft and grassy surfaces which I was reminded of with every painful step. By the 11 mile mark, I was tip-toeing over and around the rocks. Not only were new blisters forming, but my heels felt like iron rods were being driven into them as they absorbed the impact of the crushing descent.

I began running through every puddle of water I came across in order to gain some short-lived relief. Creek crossings were a glorious sight indeed! Somewhere in the last couple miles I think my feet went numb and I just tried to push as hard as I could to get the torture over with. With only 200 yards to the finish, I glanced down and noticed blood oozing out my left shoe near my pinky toe. Not good.

Upon finishing, I proceeded straight over to nearby Beaver Lake where I soaked my battered feet for about fifteen minutes in the ice cold mountain water. When it was all said and done, I ended up with 7 blisters, 2 badly bruised heels and a humbled spirit. I wouldn't run another step for over a week as I hobbled around.

Lesson learned…

Not only is it important to buy properly fitting shoes, it's also important to test those shoes on a variety of training runs and specifically on the type of terrain you'll encounter in upcoming races. I failed on both accounts as I bought the shoes online without trying them on (a great deal, I might add) and didn't test them out like I should have. Sometimes we have to learn the hard way…darn it!

Will I run this race again? Absolutely! Will I wear the same shoes? Absolutely NOT!! Next time I'll wear shoes that offer more protection and cushioning for the pounding expected.

May you learn from my mistake and have more bliss than blisters!

Chapter Ten:
Racing Flats

Shoes That Can Lead to a PR!

One of the secrets I've learned over the years is the value of using racing flats for shorter races like a 5k. Eventually, you may hit a plateau in your 5k or 10k PR (personal record). Sometimes the simplest answer is the most effective. While proper training, recovery, and race tactics are the most important factors towards running a personal best, some of the challenge can be met simply by wearing lighter running shoes.

Hence the "racing flat." Though an effective tool, these lightweight shoes are little known or untried in many running circles. The shoe is called a "flat" because it is just that-a flat, thin sole with very little heel and just enough to protect the foot from the pavement or trail.

The running shoes that the majority of people toe the line with can weigh 12 ounces or more. Flats can weigh as little as 4 ounces. Think of it this way, every time your foot lifts, it is taking the weight of the shoe with it. Save it a few ounces per step and it adds up.

A Legendary Experiment With Running Shoes

Take it from Bill Bowerman, coach of the iconic Steve Prefontaine and a legend in his own right. He claimed that for each ounce lighter a miler's shoe, this saved him 200 pounds during a race. This is the same Bill Bowerman who helped start a little company called Nike by making lightweight racing flats with the help of his wife's waffle iron.

This may sound a bit dramatic, but in practical terms the results are quite significant. Though varying conditions make it difficult to pinpoint just how much of a difference racing flats can make, a traditionally accepted theory is an improvement of one second per ounce per mile. In other words, if a runner trades in his or her 13 ounce running shoes for a 6 ounce racing flat, expected improvement would be about 21 seconds for a 5k or 42 seconds for a 10k. The improvement may be even more significant for slower runners, given the increase in time run and steps taken throughout. Not bad for just a change of shoes!

A Word of Caution

For most runners, I would not recommend extremely lightweight flats for distances above a half marathon, and even this distance should be approached with caution. There are lighter-weight running shoes that are more appropriate for the marathon, however. A marathoner switching to the 7.7 ounce Saucony Kinvara may still enjoy a 2+ minute advantage over the 26.2 mile distance.

I must caution as well that a majority of runners should employ these shoes only in races, and perhaps in a speed workout. Others may not be able to handle the lack of stability, support, and/or cushioning at all, not even for the duration of a race. I've personally experienced some Achilles pain when using racing flats for much more than races. Your 10-13 oz running shoes will provide the needed support & cushioning for your daily training runs.

Besides, racing flats are made to last a quarter to half the miles of a normal training shoe. I like to save my racing flats for race day in order to make them last longer. There's also a special feeling and positive state of mind that occurs when lacing up these feather-weight running shoes. You can feel yourself changing over to "race mode". I still recall wearing my Nike Lunaracers (6oz) for the first time in a local 5k and the sensation of my legs feeling weightless. Not surprisingly, I hit a PR that day.

Here are some of the more notable racing flats on the market...

Brooks Green Silence
Weight: 7.2 oz (size 9)

Nike Lunaracer
Weight: 6oz (size 9)

Mizuno Wave Universe 3
Weight: 3.6 oz (size 9)

New Balance MR1400
Weight: 7.1 oz (size 9)

Adidas adiZero Rocket
Weight: 7.0 oz (size 9)

Asics Piranha SP 3
Weight 4.7 oz (size 9)

Puma Complete RoadRacer 4
Weight: 7.1 oz (size 9)

Pearl Izumi Streak II
Weight: 7.6 oz (size 9)

Saucony Grid Type A4
Weight: 6.3 oz (size 9)

Zoot Ultra Speed
Weight: 7.4 oz (size 9)

Elite Runner Spotlight: Dean Karnazes

Dean Karnazes is a modern-day folk hero of sorts. The "Ultramarathon Man", as he's called, is perhaps the most inspirational runner in the world today. It was Dean who first inspired me to get off my couch in the spring of 2008 after reading his book, *Ultramarathon Man: Confessions of an All-Night Runner.* Dean will be the first to admit that he's not the fastest runner but he serves as a motivational voice to help people around the world begin putting one foot in front of the other. Still, Dean has accomplished some pretty amazing feats as a runner including...

*Winning the grueling 135 mile Badwater Ultra across Death Valley
*Running 50 marathons in 50 states in 50 straight days
*Running 350 continuous miles
*Ran nearly 3,000 miles across the country to raise funds to fight child obesity
*11-time finisher of the Western States 100 including multiple Top-10 placements
*Named one of the "Top 100 Most Influential People in the World" by *Time* magazine

Here's Dean's response to the question, *"What are 3 of the most valuable things you've learned as a runner?"*

1) There's magic in misery.
2) It doesn't matter how fast you are going if you are going in the wrong direction.
3) First or last, we all cross that same finish line.

You can learn more about Dean and follow his amazing adventures on his website…
www.UltraMarathonMan.com

Chapter Eleven:
Taking The 'Dread' Out of the Treadmill

Treadmill workouts have taken much criticism over the years as a training tool and many of those criticisms prove to be quite valid. Compared to running outdoors, the treadmill can be boring as you stare at the same wall or out the same window (or at the same TV).

By running on a moving belt, you also fail to duplicate the undulating terrain of a road or trail. The treadmill also offers a softer surface which sets you up for a rude awakening come race day when you have to negotiate the asphalt of a road race or the rocks and roots of a trail race. Treadmill training also fails to factor in weather changes such as wind speed and temperature fluctuation.

A Few Positive Treadmill Workout Uses...

While I agree that doing all of our training on the treadmill would be detrimental, I still believe there's a place for solid treadmill workouts. Most of our training should simulate the course conditions of the race we've signed up for but let's face it, there are times when that just isn't possible. If you live in the flatlands of Kansas and you've signed up for the Pike's Peak Marathon where you'll have to climb 7,815 feet with an average 11% grade, you have a small dilemma on your hands. Though you can't simulate the altitude of the race, you're able to set your treadmill at an 11% grade which will be very helpful.

If you live in a region that gets its fair share of snow during the winter, you know there are days when doing a hard tempo run outdoors is nearly impossible due to the difficulty of tromping through that white stuff. The treadmill is a handy tool to use in this circumstance as you set the speed to your tempo of preference.

Here's another clever use of the treadmill I recently came across:

http://running.competitor.com/2011/05/news/man-training-for-badwater-in-homemade-heat-room_27560

3 Proven Treadmill Workouts

The following are three treadmill workouts I've found to be beneficial when outdoor conditions are less than ideal...

Hills On The Mill Challenge (30 minutes)

Speeds in parentheses serve as examples

First 10 minutes - Warm-up with your normal easy pace (7.0 at 0% grade)

Minute 11 - Increase speed one notch and increase grade to 1% (7.1 at 1% grade)

Minute 12 - Increase speed one notch and increase grade to 2% (7.2 at 2% grade)

Minute 13 - Increase speed one notch and increase grade to 3% (7.3 at 3% grade)

Minute 14 - Increase speed one notch and increase grade to 4% (7.4 at 4% grade)

Minute 15 - Increase speed one notch and increase grade to 5% (7.5 at 5% grade)

Minute 16 - Increase speed one notch and increase grade to 5.5% (7.6 at 5.5% grade)

Minute 17 - Increase speed one notch and increase grade to 6% (7.7 at 6% grade)

Minute 18 - Increase speed one notch and increase grade to 6.5% (7.8 at 6.5% grade)

Minute 19 - Increase speed one notch and increase grade to 7% (7.9 at 7% grade)

Minute 20 - Increase speed one notch and increase grade to 7.5% (8.0 at 7.5% grade)

*Last 10 minutes - Cool down with your normal easy pace & 0% grade (7.0 at 0%)

This is a very challenging treadmill workout that should only be done 2-3 times each month. You should be able to gradually increase speed and grade as your legs & lungs adjust to the hills. You'll know you're overdoing it when you have lingering soreness in the Achilles area. With time, you'll hit 10% grade and higher.

Speed Mill Challenge (38-50 minutes)

Speeds in parentheses serve as examples. The grade will stay at 0%

*First 10 minutes - Warm-up with your normal easy pace (7.0)

*Next 3 minutes - Your tempo pace (8.5)

*Next 3 minutes - Your 5k race pace (10.0)

*Repeat(tempo & 5k) 3-5 times based on your fitness level

*Finish with 10 minutes of cool down at your easy pace (7.0)

This workout proves that running on the treadmill doesn't have to be boring. One of the great aspects of the treadmill is the constant pace you're forced to maintain, even when the mind tells you to slow down. On the track, it becomes easier to slow down your pace when fatigue begins to set in during those later repeats. This challenging speed session is excellent for leg turnover.

Long Run Progression Challenge
(90 minutes)

Speeds in parentheses serve as examples. The grade will stay at 0%

*First 20 minutes - Warm-up with your normal easy pace (7.0)

*Next 15 minutes - 1 min/mi slower than your 5k pace (8.5)

*Next 5 minutes - Recover with easy pace (7.0)

*Next 10 minutes - 30 sec/mi slower than your 5k pace (9.2)

*Next 5 minutes - Recover with easy pace (7.0)

*Next 10 minutes - 20 sec/mi slower than your 5k pace (9.5)

*Next 5 minutes - Recover with easy pace (7.0)

*Next 5 minutes - 5k pace (10.0)

*Last 15 minutes - Cool down with your easy pace (7.0)

This may seem like a long time on the treadmill and it certainly is. But you'll reap tremendous benefits by completing this workout practiced by the Team USA Minnesota runners during their brutal winters. This treadmill workout will teach the body how to "feel" the various paces required in races from 5k to half-marathon.

If you're going to fire up the belt, do it sparingly but effectively!

Chapter Twelve:
Tabata Training

Short...But Truly Sweet

Have you heard of Tabata training? If you're short on time and looking for some training that yields the most bang for the buck, look no further than Tabata. Tabata training, named after Dr. Izumi Tabata, goes back to a 1996 study in Japan where subjects alternated between 20 seconds of ultra-intense exercise followed by 10 seconds of rest and repeated continuously for 4 minutes or 8 cycles.

If a Tabata regimen is done correctly, one word will quickly begin to rise to the surface...pain! This method can be applied to any form of exercise but for our purposes, we'll focus on utilizing Tabata in running.

Tabata intervals should only be attempted by runners who are fit and have some recent interval experience (i.e. 200m, 400m, 800m).

*Note: *Due to its high intensity level, Tabata should only be done once per week in the beginning. You may even want to consult a physician beforehand. After a few months, you can increase to twice a week.*

I prefer doing Tabata intervals at my local track. If you don't have access to a local track, find a road with minimal traffic. This workout is not only intense, it requires extreme focus and discipline as you pay attention to your watch.

With Tabata Training Always...

Begin with a 1-2 mile warm-up of light running. Normally, I recommend stretching after a workout but in the case of Tabata, I recommend some light stretching immediately after the 1-2 mile warm-up. The Tabata routine goes like this...

- **Push very hard for 20 seconds (pretty much 100% effort)**
- **Rest for 10 seconds**
- **Repeat this eight times**

You should be feeling pretty taxed by the third or fourth interval but this is where the real "fun" begins as you push through the pain. It's crucial to stay tuned to your watch, especially as your body tries to encourage you to rest longer than 10 seconds before beginning the next interval. This short rest/hard run cycle is pure magic in multiple ways. Upon completing the last interval, finish with another mile of cool down running before stretching.

Tabata Training...

- **Increases Strength** - you're building those fast twitch muscle fibers
- **Increases Cardiovascular endurance** - sustained discomfort with short rest
- **Increases Anaerobic capacity** - no other form of training compares in this area
- **Increases VO2 Max** - the maximum capacity of the body to transport oxygen for use
- **Teaches your body to recover quickly** and remove metabolic waste products more efficiently
- **Improves running economy** - how efficiently a person uses oxygen while running at a given pace

As you incorporate Tabata training into your workouts, you're sure to see your body reach a new level of fitness and speed in a short amount of time. If you find that you're unable to make it to 4 minutes, stop at 2 minutes and slowly build up.

If you don't look like this after the workout, you simply didn't push hard enough...

You say potato...I say Tabata!

Elite Runner Spotlight: Sage Canaday

Sage Canaday has experienced success in road, trail and mountain races throughout the United States and abroad. After competing in track and cross country for Cornell University, Sage went on to train with the Hanson's-Brooks Distance Project team as an elite runner for 2 ½ years. He's written a book about his Hanson's experience titled, *Running For the Hansons*, available on Amazon. Sage's resume includes...

Personal Bests:
*5k – 14:29
*10k - 29:47
*10 miles – 49:01
*Half Marathon – 1:04:32
*Marathon – 2:16:52

Highlights:
*2-time Olympic Trials qualifier in the marathon
*Course record at the White River 50 mile (6:16)
*American record at the Mt. Washington Road Race (58:26)
*2012 USA Mountain Running Champion

Here's Sage's response to the question, *"What are 3 of the most valuable things you've learned as a runner?"*

1.) Take your easy days easy. Every day you train has a purpose and when you need to really recover from a hard workout or race you can almost never run too slow. Most people are too eager to push, push, push every day and they end up injured and/or over-trained as a result. Slow down

71

and enjoy some runs - let your body tell you what to do!

2.) The race is never over until it's over. Dramatic things can happen near the end of long races and you can't rest on your laurels until you actually cross that finish line. On the flip-side, if you are racing a competitor and they are too far ahead and out of sight there is still a chance you can catch them late in the race. Never give up!

3.) You must enjoy the process of training. If you want to stay with the sport long-term you can't let any single bad races or tough workouts define who you are as a runner (you also can't expect to race well and feel good all the time). You must roll with the punches and be flexible. You've got to enjoy your runs and have fun spending your time and energy in such an endeavor if you want to be in it for the long run.

You can follow Sage's running at his website...
www.SageCanaday.com

or his YouTube channel...
www.YouTube.com/Vo2maxProductions

Photo Credit: Kevin Jantzer

Chapter Thirteen
Building Endurance:

Are You In For The Long Run?

From the 5k to the marathon, one of the most essential ingredients to improving overall endurance running is the long run. And what is endurance? Let's see what Webster's has to say:

en·dur·ance:

> the ability to withstand hardship or adversity; especially : the ability to sustain a prolonged stressful effort or activity

> the act or an instance of enduring or suffering

Those definitions are certainly relevant for runners of all distances. One of our primary goals is to increase the amount of time we're able to hold a specific pace. In other words, you might easily be able to run a mile in 7 minutes, but how about holding that pace for 3.1 miles, 10 miles or 13.1 miles? It doesn't really matter how much speed you have if you can't cover the distance of whatever race you're running.

What is the Long Run?

The long run, or endurance running, is simply the longest training run of the week, both in miles and length of time. Depending on experience, someone training for a 5k will need to cover 6 to 12 miles on their long runs. I began to notice significant improvement when I consistently included a long run in my weekly training plan. Before I became serious about lowering my 5k times, I found myself settling for shorter runs as I reasoned that "it's only a 5k I'm training for." If I was crunched for time, I would simply cut miles off my long run thinking it was no big deal. Since then, I've discovered it is a BIG deal.

Finally Passing a Rival

Race after race I would run against him. Race after race he would beat me. His name is Joe Baker. It didn't matter if I was ahead of him for 95% of the race. Joe would manage to overtake me in that last 5%. It was frustrating and I knew something had to change.

After all, if you do what you've always done, you'll get what you've always got. Albert Einstein had a definition for insanity: "Doing the same thing over and over again but expecting a different result." I tend to agree with Mr. Einstein, especially when it comes to running.

Around the peak of my frustration with losing to Joe, I was invited by a group of guys to join them on their weekly long run. It was January in northwest Ohio which meant it was freezing cold and there was snow on the ground. We did these long runs at one of the Toledo metro parks which contained miles of trails.

Each week, we would cover 10-14 miles at 9min/mile pace. We certainly weren't breaking any records but I began to notice improvement after just three or four of these long runs. I was able to run longer without becoming as winded. My day of putting these long runs and endurance running to the test would come at a 5k race in mid-February where I again found myself standing on the starting line with Joe Baker. The air was cool & crisp but the course was about ready to be burned up.

The gun fired and we were off. The first mile was fairly tame as neither of us really wanted to lead but by the midway point, Joe made his move. He proceeded to put a gap of about 15 yards between us as we hit the two mile mark. With less than ½ mile to go, I pulled even and began a surge that gave me a 15 yard lead of my own. I could smell the finish line yet I knew Joe would put forth one final kick. But amazingly, with less than 100 yards to go and the finish line in sight, Joe was now 50 yards behind me and losing more ground with every step I took. That final kick by Joe never happened. Sweet victory was mine as I crossed the line in 19:15 with Joe coming in at 19:26.

Joe congratulated me upon finishing and we enjoyed some usual post-race conversation. Since that day, the gap between Joe and I has continued to widen as I've continued to progress and become more consistent in my training.

If there's one key ingredient that pushed me past Joe it's my endurance running or what most call, the long run. I had known for a while that Joe seldom runs more than 20 miles total for the week and his longest training runs are 4 or 5 miles. To his credit, Joe is gifted with natural speed and back in his prime, he was churning out 16 minute 5ks. Since 98% of all the races Joe runs are 5k, he hasn't seen the need to include a long run in his weekly training. But without that long run, Joe continues to sacrifice endurance...that ability to hold a given pace for a longer period of time.

Benefits of the Long Run

1. Using fat as fuel - As we've mentioned in the nutrition section, our bodies will use carbohydrates as the first option for fuel. After carb stores are depleted, the body then moves into using fat stores as fuel. This is a wonderful thing, especially for those of you trying to lose those stubborn excess pounds. Incorporating a long run into your training can be a healthy weight loss tool.

2. Glycogen storage increases - When glycogen stores are depleted, muscles are stimulated to restock to a higher level. This is a survival mechanism the body uses to ensure it doesn't run out of glycogen again. Simply put, by gradually increasing the distance of your long runs, you'll gradually increase your glycogen storage. Remember, glycogen is the fuel our muscles crave!

3. Increased capillary density - Endurance running increases the number of capillaries per muscle cell, which improves the efficiency of oxygen and nutrient delivery as well as the removal of carbon dioxide and other waste products. More capillaries equal more oxygen & nutrients to our muscle cells.

4. Muscle fiber adaptations - Though the 5k requires some fast twitch muscle fiber action for pure speed, it also requires slow twitch action in order to sustain pace. Slow twitch fibers naturally have more mitochondria, more aerobic enzyme activity, more oxidative capacity, and more capillaries than fast twitch fibers. Endurance running will not actually build new slow twitch fiber but it will give the existing fast twitch fibers some of the same qualities as slow twitch fibers. Some people (Usain Bolt) are born with more fast twitch fiber and some people (Ryan Hall) are born with more slow twitch fiber.

Long Run Pace

A general rule of thumb for your long run pace is 1 ½ to 2 minutes slower than 5k race pace. For example, if you can hold a 7 minute per mile 5k pace, your long run pace will be 8:30 to 9 minutes per mile. Beginners should stay closer to the 2 minutes slower pace until their bodies adjust to the miles. Doing long runs with someone of similar ability and speed can provide motivation and conversation along the way. Afterward, you can reward yourselves with a hearty breakfast or lunch.

Run With a Group

Finding a group to do your long run with can be an incredible motivator. For those who live in an area where winters are harsh, finding a group can sometimes mean the difference between staying in bed and getting out the door. When it's 25 degrees and windy, it's very easy to blow off a long run when you're planning to run solo.

For you extroverts, doing your long run with a group can provide added incentive as you look forward to 2-3 hours of conversation with friends. And with a long run, you're more likely to find other runners who can sustain the slower pace without much difficulty. I'm amazed at how fast the time flies by when running with a group. There's been many times when I've looked down at my watch for the first time to see that we've already clicked off 10, 11 or 12 miles. On the other hand, I've had many solo long runs where I look down at my watch several times only to see that I've run less than 5 miles

Some runners enjoy doing all their runs with a partner or group. Others prefer the solitude of simply hearing their own footsteps. If you're the solitary type, I still encourage you to try the group experience in an upcoming long run.

Building Endurance for the Long Run

Are you ready to start holding a faster pace longer with every race you run? Are you ready to see your endurance level increase dramatically? Are you ready to train your body to burn fat as fuel and lose those extra pounds weighing you down?

What are you waiting for? It's time to go long!

CJ's Lessons Learned...
Biting Off More Than I Could Chew

As I mentioned in the beginning, I picked up running again in the spring of 2008 after almost twenty years away from it. After finishing *Ultramarathon Man: Confessions of an All Night Runner* by Dean Karnazes, I was ready to start training for a 100 miler! No sweat, right? I remember how humbled I was after running 6 miles for the first time. After that outing along a treacherous Ohio highway shoulder, I decided to tone down the "100 mile zeal" a bit by signing up for a 50k trail race (31 miles) and a road marathon.

At this point, it was the end of April. The 50k trail race was scheduled for the 3rd weekend in August and the road marathon would be the last weekend of September. Did I mention these would be the very first races I would be running after a 20 year running break? Let's just skip the 5k, 5 mile, 10k, 10 mile, half-marathon, etc.

I weighed nearly 30 pounds more than I do now and had absolutely no clue what I was doing. No plan, no coach, no real rhyme or reason in my training. Just head out the door and see what happens. I was a decent basketball player so I just figured I'd naturally get the hang of this running gig. How hard could it be?

Carnage on the Potawatomi Trail...

By the time the Silver Lake 50k arrived on August 23, the longest training run I had managed was 18 miles. Now I had to run 31 miles on one of the toughest trails in the Midwest...the vaunted "Potto" trail in Pinckney, Michigan.

What's another 13 miles?

When the gun fired at 7am it was 70 degrees with 80% humidity. There were over 40 brave souls who shuffled off into the woods and another 25 in the 50 mile race on the same trail. By the 18 mile mark (coincidence?) of this brutal course, I was a walking zombie. Turn out the lights, the party's over. My legs refused to turn over any faster than a 13 minute-per-mile death shuffle over the last 10 miles. It's a scary feeling to be in that kind of misery with so far to go.

5 hours 31 minutes later, I crossed the finish line in 92 degree heat with 85% humidity. I was thoroughly defeated and humbled. What are those famous words we utter after outings like these?

"Never again."

Oh, but wait. Remember that road marathon I signed up for? It was now a month away and the dread washed over me as I anticipated it while slouched in a lawn chair. I'm not sure I ran one step during the week after the 50k. When would the soreness in my legs subside? Did I do permanent damage? Was the road marathon even an option?

Carnage in Akron and Beyond...

September 27th arrived sooner than I would have liked. My body was still having a hard time forgiving me for what I had put it through the previous month. The gun fired and over 3,000 of us began our journey. My goal was to run a sub 3hr 30min race. Things were on pace until that mystical 18 mile mark (seeing a theme here?). It was then that I began to experience the dreaded cramping in the hamstrings. *"Nooo...not now!!"*

I thought I'd done a fairly good job of fluid intake. Nonetheless, I was forced to pull over to the side of the road and stretch. At this point, both hamstrings began to seize up into grape fruit-sized knots and I was in shear agony. Seeing my discomfort, a kind police officer came over to see if he could help and offered me his bottle of water since I was between fluid stations. After what seemed like 10 minutes, I thanked him and began attempting to run. Imagine someone trying to run with two stiff, straight legs and you'll have an accurate picture of what I must have looked like. Spectators probably gasped as I hobbled by. Haile Gebrselassie's marathon world record was certainly safe today.

Eventually, my stride loosened up and the cramping eased, though not completely. It was a great feeling to finish inside the Akron University football stadium where thousands of friends & family members awaited their loved ones. After all was said and done, I crossed the finish line in 3 hours 45 minutes.

Again, I was humbled. Again, I uttered those famous post-race words...*never again.* Did I learn my lesson? You be the judge...a few days later, I signed up for the November 6th Lithia Loop Trail Marathon in Ashland, Oregon. Again, I suffered. A few days after that race, I signed up for the December 5th Tecumseh Trail Marathon in Bloomington, Indiana.

Again, I suffered-this time in 24 degree weather while running in 2-3 inches of fresh snow. Had my sanity returned after this outing? It took one more "pain and torture" fest before I finally got the hint. The race that finally broke me completely was the Way Too Cool 50k in Cool, California the following March. I sometimes refer to it as the Way Too "Cruel" 50k.

Lesson Learned…

Something finally sank in after running that last "cruel" race in March 2009. My training was not only woefully deficient but I wasn't exposing my body to the kind of rigorous terrain I would encounter at many of these races. For example, I lived in Findlay, Ohio at the time where it was flat as a pancake. The Way Too Cool 50k contains a significant amount of downhill that can grind a person's quads into hamburger if they haven't practiced downhill running. Sure enough, my quads were finished in that race by the halfway point. I simply didn't have access to that kind of downhill terrain.

From that point forward, I decided not to sign up for races in which I couldn't properly train on similar course terrain & grade. I would do a much better job researching the course layout and knowing the specifics of things like fluid stations, course markings and elevation gain/loss. If I was going to continue this wonderful sport of running, I owed it to myself (and my body) to learn from my failures and also to glean knowledge and wisdom from more experienced runners.

A nutritional lesson learned…

In the Silver Lake 50k race, I broke one of the cardinal rules in the area of nutrition…

Thou shalt not introduce thy digestive system to a new food or drink on race day!

Have you ever looked inside your race bag of sponsor goodies and decided to try something in there for the first time…on race day? This is precisely what I did a few minutes before this torturous 50k was to begin. Inside the race bag, I found a *Clif Shot* "Double Espresso" flavored gel.

I thought to myself, *"Mmm, I need all the energy I can get going into this race."* I quickly downed the 100 calorie pouch and almost immediately felt the caffeine coursing through my veins. Unfortunately, my stomach would protest about 30 minutes later, having never experienced this flavor previously. Talk about high octane fuel!

It's a good idea to stick with fueling sources that your body has been used to using during training. It's also a good idea to find out ahead of time what the aid stations in your races will offer in terms of food & fluid. If *Gatorade* will be served, you may want to practice using *Gatorade* in the weeks leading up to race day. How about gels? Will the race have *GU*? *Hammer*? *Clif*? Your other option would be to bring your own food or fluid of choice and have a friend or family member hand it to you at various points along the race course. Either way, try to eliminate as many surprises as possible on your big day. After all, you've trained too hard to have something like nutrition ruin your race.

Chapter Fourteen:
Just For The "Hill" of It

Running Up That Hill

When we used to live in northwest Ohio, finding a good hill to run wasn't easy but not impossible either. Perhaps the same rings true in your neck of the woods. Now I live in Colorado Springs where finding a "hill" is as simple as looking out my front window (Pikes Peak to name one).

Why a Hill Run?

The best runners all agree that there is no better way to build strength in every aspect of our running than incorporating hills into our training. Runners at every level want to improve...they want to get faster. But how?

The simple answer is to find a hill. Then run up it, run down it, run fast, run slow, run long, run short. Run that hill and keep running it until it's no longer a question of getting faster but of how fast you want to become.

It's force, not speed that builds muscle strength. We can run fast reps on the track until the cows come home but we won't improve our strength the way running up hills can. Muscles are made up of various fibers (muscle cells) and there are three types of these fibers we can build by running hills...

1. Slow twitch - Distance runners have lots of slow twitch fibers. These fibers produce less force than the other two but they work aerobically and they

take a long time to tire out. This is what makes
them perfect for endurance events.

2. Intermediate twitch - Middle distance runners
   (800m to mile) have lots of intermediate muscle
   fibers which make for long powerful strides.

3. Fast twitch - Sprinters (400m & shorter) have a
   larger percentage of fast twitch fibers which
   produce the most force of all. But since they only
   work anaerobically, they're only good for short
   bursts of running.

We can build all three types of muscle fiber by simply
running hills, including a hill run in our training.

Getting Started

Before beginning any hill run workout, it's essential that
you do 1-2 miles of easy running to get the muscles
warmed up. Following the easy warm-up, it's good to do
several strides of 100 meters or less to get the legs
prepared. These are run at 70-80% of your maximum
effort.

Now that you've properly warmed up, you're ready to
decide on your hill run workout. Here are five hill run
workouts to choose from when hill training…

Long Hill Runs

Nothing works better than a long run that includes a long
hill to build slow twitch muscle fibers. Start easy and
incorporate a ½ to 1 mile of moderately steep uphill
within your longer run and only do this every second or
third week. As your fitness improves, up that total to 2-3
miles and keep the pace easy. Remember, by simply
running up a hill, we're increasing the force demands on
the muscles. Going too hard too soon will increase the

amount of recovery time needed for the next quality workout.

Long Hill Run Repeats

To strengthen all our intermediate fibers, we need to up the force and intensity. That's where long hill repeats come in. Depending on our fitness, we should start with 4-8 thirty second repetitions of the same hill and gradually increase the duration of our repeats with each workout session until we reach a maximum of 90 seconds for each repeat. We want to work hard enough to force our intermediate fibers into action but not so fast that we recruit the fast twitch fibers.

For recovery between reps, jog back down to the base of the hill then walk until your total rest period is 2-3 minutes for shorter reps and 4-5 minutes for longer ones. Finish this workout feeling as if you had another rep or two in you.

Short Hill Run Repeats

Short hill run repeats are the best workout there is for strengthening our fast twitch fibers. They also recruit a wider range of muscle fiber which we then incorporate into our stride.

These repeats run on steep, short hills give the runner a smoother, faster stride when it comes to cranking out that faster race time. We're talking 40-60 meters in terms of distance or 8-10 seconds in terms of time.

Remember, this workout isn't about endurance. We're generating enough force to get our fast twitch fibers jumping. We can't sustain that for very long and we shouldn't. A good indicator that you've overdone it with these short but sweet repeats is above average pain in the Achilles or Soleus (lower calf).

You'll want to run each repeat at 90-95% effort or just under an all-out sprint. Start with 4-5 reps then build up over several sessions to 8-12 reps. At the top, turn and walk back to the start then rest 2-3 minutes before starting your next rep.

Trust me, you'll want to take the full rest!

Hill Springing & Bounding Hill Run Techniques

Think back to your childhood days when you were into skipping. It's really as simple as that when it comes to what the great New Zealand running coach Arthur Lydiard referred to as "springing."

These can be done on a moderate grade hill (not the steepest) such as the one you use for longer hill repeats. In high skipping or springing, you'll have the same motion as a regular skip, but you'll drive the knees a bit higher than normal. At the top of the hill, turn and jog back down to the start, wait 1 minute and begin the next rep. 2-3 reps of these are fine.

"Bounding" is another technique drill you can incorporate into running up that hill. Think Michael "Air" Jordan on these. You simply drive off one foot, hover in the air like "His Airness" and land on the opposite foot, immediately initiating another bound forward. Again, 2-3 reps are fine and could even be done as the last couple reps in a long hill run repeat workout.

Downhill Strides

Think of these as quad busters. When running downhill fast, our quads have to contract and relax at the same time. This puts a huge stress on our muscle fibers which results in fiber damage which leads to some nasty soreness a couple days later. The good news is that the soreness actually triggers a response in our body that prevents future quad soreness as well as rebuilding those muscles much stronger than before. I'm actually experiencing some quad soreness even as I write this.

When you get to the bottom of that hill, you'll want to walk or lightly jog back up to the top and then start again. Start with a couple of these and work up to 4-5 reps. Your quads will thank you later.

Finishing Up...

Following a hill workout, it's important to get another 1-2 miles of easy cool down running on some flatter terrain.

No matter where you live, you should be able to find some hills, even if low grade. If you do live in a flatter area, you can translate some of the workouts above on a treadmill.

An example of a moderate hill would be 4-6% grade and a steep hill would be 7% and above. Adjust speed based on fitness level and the above workout descriptions.

Because these hill run workouts are so physically demanding, you don't want to run more than one or two hill sessions of any kind in a single week and only run hills 2-3 weeks per month in the beginning.

With that said, you'll want to remain consistent in running up those hills in order to build the different muscle fibers. By doing this, I guarantee your race times will improve - from the mile to the marathon. So go ahead and get started...

Just for the "hill" of it!

A Training Glimpse
6 Weeks Leading Up to my 5k Personal Best

This is not a 5k training program for a beginner. However, here's a glimpse into what my 6 weeks of training looked like leading up to my 5k personal best (17:40) that I achieved at the Express Fall 5k in Findlay, OH on September 17th, 2011. This was nearly 3 ½ years after I started running again. Since then, we've moved to Colorado Springs where it's been more difficult to get near that time due to having less oxygen at 6500 feet elevation. Still, I'm not ruling out the possibility of pushing through to a new personal best with proper training and continued improvement as a runner.

6 Weeks out
Mon 8/8/11
*Morning - 14x400m with 200m jogs (5:24/mi avg. pace), 1.5mi warm up & cool down
*Evening – 2mi easy at local reservoir with wife Shelley
Tues 8/9/11 – 7.1mi at Findlay reservoir (8:40/mi avg. pace)
Wed 8/10/11 – 6.12mi at Emory Adams Park (7:37/mi avg. pace)
Thurs 8/11/11 – 6mi at Second Sole group run (7:32/mi avg. pace)
Fri 8/12/11 – Rest
Sat 8/13/11 – Up Up Away 5k race – 17:46 (new PR), 2mi warm up, 2.5mi cool down
Sun 8/14/11 – 6.57mi at Findlay Reservoir (7:21/mi avg. pace)
Total = 43.5 miles

5 Weeks out
Mon 8/15/11 – 8.07mi on West River Rte (7:11/mi avg. pace, middle miles at 6:28 pace)

Tues 8/16/11 – 4x800m at Donnell track (5:52/mi avg. pace) – 2mi warm & cool

Wed 8/17/11 – 3.07mi in neighborhood (7:23/mi avg. pace)

Thurs 8/18/11 – 6.02mi at Second Sole group run (7:40/mi avg. pace)

Fri 8/19/11 – Pemberville 5mi race – 30:27, 2mi warm & cool

Sat 8/20/11 – 11.41mi at Findlay Reservoir (7:47/mi avg. pace)

Sun 8/21/11 – 7.36mi down S. Main (7:51/mi avg. pace)

Total = 51.34 miles

4 Weeks out

Mon 8/22/11 – 8mi on West River Rte (7:20/mi avg. pace)

Tues 8/23/11 – 6x800m w/400m jogs, 2x200m (5:27/mi avg. pace), 2.5mi warm & cool

Wed 8/24/11 – 7.17mi on West River Rte (7:44/mi avg. pace)

Thurs 8/25/11 – 6mi at Second Sole group run (6:40/mi avg. pace, 6:24 last mile)

Fri 8/26/11 – 6.32mi in neighborhood (7:47/mi avg. pace)

Sat 8/27/11 – 12mi with Strider running club (7:40/mi avg. pace)

Sun 8/28/11 – Rest

Total = 46.99 miles

3 Weeks out

Mon 8/29/11 – Tempo progression on Donnell track – 1.5mi in 9:00, 1mi in 5:37, 800m in 2:46, 400m in 1:18 4mi warm & cool

Tues 8/30/11 – 8.51mi in neighborhood (7:41/mi avg. pace)

Wed 8/31/11 – 5.6mi with eastside group (7:37/mi avg. pace)

Thurs 9/1/11 – 8.51mi at Second Sole group run (7:02/mi avg. pace)

Fri 9/2/11 – 4.15mi in neighborhood (7:39/mi avg. pace)

Sat 9/3/11 – 14.05mi with Strider running club (7:27/mi avg.

Sun 9/4/11 – 6.76mi on West River Rte (7:46/mi avg. pace)
Total = 55.08 miles

2 Weeks out
Mon 9/5/11 – 16x400m w/200m jogs (5:24/mi avg. for each), 4mi warm & cool
Tues 9/6/11 – 9.47mi on West River Rte (7:29/mi avg. pace)
Wed 9/7/11 – 7mi **fartlek at Emory Adams Park (7:10/mi avg. pace)
Thurs 9/8/11 – 5.98mi at Second Sole group run (7:07/mi avg. pace)
Fri 9/9/11 – 2.56mi in neighborhood (7:45/mi avg. pace)
Sat 9/10/11 – Kalida Pioneer 5k race – 17:52, 4mi warm & cool
Sun 9/11/11 – 8.92mi north on country roads (7:30/mi avg. pace)
Total = 50.05 miles

**The word *fartlek* is a Swedish term meaning "speed play." It's a fun way to work some speed into a training run. Simply look ahead at an object (i.e. sign, telephone pole, tree, etc.) and run at 90% effort or faster. Once you reach the object, run a couple minutes easy before picking another object ahead which might vary from 100 meters to 800 meters ahead. The neat thing about a fartlek is that you choose how far and how fast.

Week of target 5k race
Mon 9/12/11 – 6mi in neighborhood (7:32/mi avg. pace)
Tues 9/13/11 – 8.06mi at Emory Adams park (3x1mi at 5:49 avg. pace)
Wed 9/14/11 – 6.6mi at Findlay Reservoir (7:50/mi avg. pace)
Thurs 9/15/11 – 4.01mi at Second Sole group run (7:25/mi avg. pace)
Fri 9/16/11 – 3.14mi in neighborhood (7:06/mi avg. pace)

Sat 9/17/11 – **Express Fall 5k Race – 17:40 (new PR!!)**, 2.5mi warm-up, no cool down
Mile 1 = 5:40, Mile 2 = 5:43, Mile 3 = 5:48, last .1mi = 30 seconds
Sun 9/18/11 – 10.11mi in neighborhood (7:25/mi avg. pace)
Total = 43.54 miles

Final Thoughts on My 5k PR...

As you can see from my weeks leading up to my 5k personal best, I didn't exactly take it easy every week. I enjoy doing races, not only for the camaraderie and competition, but also as a way to get a speed workout. Even though I ran several races in the weeks before, I had September 17 circled on my calendar as a target race for a new personal best. Some of my deciding factors included...

*Flat point-to-point course with no turn around
*Accurately measured course I was able to run ahead of time to confirm accuracy
*The chance of a nice, cool mid-Sept morning for racing – weather was high 40s with no wind or precipitation...perfect racing conditions!
*Less than 3 miles from where I was living which meant more sleep & short drive

There are many factors that go into a training program. What works for one person, may not be the answer for another. But as you look down through those 6 weeks in my training, you'll notice I was pretty consistent with incorporating a long run and some sort of speed workout (repeats, tempo) each week. These are non-negotiable for anyone looking to see continued improvement and to reach your potential in any race.

Conclusion

Running has taken countless people to places they would have never gone otherwise. How can merely putting one foot in front of the other be so invigorating, freeing and inspiring at the same time? Only those who are willing to give running a try will experience the many physical, emotional and social benefits that it yields.

Doug Ordway, a northwest Ohio runner still clocking low 18 minute 5ks into his late 50s, once told me that a person who's taken a long layoff from running can expect to reasonably see improvement over the course of up to 10 years after picking it up again. If this is true, I can expect to see some of my best times into my 40s which is very encouraging. Here's an article on the Ordway family of runners:
http://www.runnersworld.com/elite-runners/daytons-ordway-family-qualifies-three-trials

Derek Turnbull was a New Zealand farmer who took up running in his early 40s and went on to set numerous age group records that still stand today in the 65-69 category including 2:41:57 in the marathon, 34:42 in the 10k, 16:38 in the 5k, 9:47 in the 3k and 4:56 in the mile.

Ed Whitlock, an 81 year-old Canadian who holds numerous 70-74, 75-79 and 80-84 age group records, started running in his 40s after quitting in his teen years. He's the only person in history who's run a sub 3 hour marathon past the age of 70, having run 2:54:48 at age 73.

Pete Magill, who writes a regular Master's column for *Running Times*, showed potential as a high school runner and even ran a year in college before giving it up.

After years of drinking, smoking and gaining weight, Magill decided to get back into running at age 40. He said it took a year just to work the smoke out of his lungs and actually feel "comfortable" running again. Since then, Magill has tapped into a fountain of youth as he continues to set master's age group records himself. He's the oldest American to have broken 15 minutes for a 5k, having run 14:45 a few months before his 50th birthday! Just recently, he ran his first half-marathon in a blazing 1:10:19.

How about you? How far will you go to tap into your potential? The reality is that most of us will not go on to set world records but it's exciting to think about breaking through to new personal bests over the course of several years after a long layoff. Whether you're running for the first time in your 20s or your 50s, there are some great years ahead of you!

Running For Pure Enjoyment

Just getting out the door provides opportunities for one adventure after another. It's a chance to breathe in fresh air, get the blood pumping and stir up the endorphins that create that "runner's high." It's an opportunity to enjoy nature in all its splendor, whether you're running in the calm of a winter snowfall or along a beautiful beach on a 75 degree sunny day.

No matter what your age or level of experience, we can all enjoy this most simple of sports. How many other sports can beginners and elites toe the line at the same time? How many other sports can a person enjoy success as a teenager and later as an 81 year-old? There's a beauty and simplicity that running embodies.

Though not an exhaustive resource, my hope is that this book has helped point you in the right direction and to also whet your appetite to learn and explore more in the areas of nutrition and training for running success.

As you endeavor to start off on the right foot, may you run with joy and gratitude with each stride you're able to take for many years to come!

Appendix:
Inspiration and Motivation for Runners

As runners, we all need a little inspiration and motivation from time to time. I encourage you to start your own list of favorite running quotes and refer to it from time to time. Words are powerful!

Some of my Favorites...

"Most people run a race to see who is fastest. I run a race to see who has the most guts." **- Steve Prefontaine**

"It hurts up to a point and then it doesn't get any worse." **- Ann Trason**

"I'm going to go out a winner if I have to find a high school race to win my last race." **- Johnny Gray, 1992 800m Bronze Medalist**

"The woods are lovely dark and deep, but I have promises to keep, and miles to go before I sleep, and miles to go before I sleep." **- Robert Frost**

"I've always felt that long, slow distance produces long, slow runners." **- Sebastian Coe**

"The will to win means nothing without the will to prepare." - **Juma Ikangaa, 1989 NYC Marathon winner**

"In running, it doesn't matter whether you come in first, in the middle of the pack, or last. You can say, 'I have finished.' There is a lot of satisfaction in that." - **Fred Lebow, New York City Marathon co-founder**

"The miracle isn't that I finished. The miracle is that I had the courage to start." - **John Bingham**

"Whether you believe you can or believe you can't, you're probably right." - **Henry Ford**

"Keep varying the program. Your body will tell you what to do." - **Joan Benoit Samuelson**

"I had as many doubts as anyone else. Standing on the starting line, we're all cowards." - **Alberto Salazar, three-time winner of the NYC marathon**

"When it's pouring rain and you're bowling along through the wet, there's satisfaction in knowing you're out there and the others aren't." - **Peter Snell**

"Mental will is a muscle that needs exercise, just like the muscles of the body." - **Lynn Jennings**

"No one ever drowned in sweat." - **Author Unknown**

"There's no such thing as bad weather, just soft people." - **Bill Bowerman**

"Those who think they have no time for bodily exercise will sooner or later have to find time for illness." - **Edward Stanley**

"Methinks that the moment my legs began to move, my thoughts began to flow." - **Henry David Thoreau**

"If you run, you are a runner. It doesn't matter how fast or how far. It doesn't matter if today is your first day or if you've been running for twenty years. There is no test to pass, no license to earn, no membership card to get. You just run." - **John Bingham**

"I often hear someone say I'm not a real runner. We are all runners, some just run faster than others. I never met a fake runner." - **Bart Yasso**

"We all have dreams. But in order to make dreams come into reality, it takes an awful lot of determination, dedication, self-discipline, and effort." - **Jesse Owens**

"I'm going to work so that it's a pure guts race at the end, and if it is, I am the only one who can win it." - **Steve Prefontaine**

"To give anything less than your best is to sacrifice the gift." - **Steve Prefontaine**

"The answer to the big questions in running is the same as the answer to the big questions in life: do the best with what you've got." - **Author Unknown**

"No one can say, 'You must not run faster than this, or jump higher than that.' The human spirit is indomitable." - **Sir Roger Bannister**

"For me, as for so many runners, there really are no finish lines. Runs end; running doesn't." - **Dean Karnazes, Author of Ultramarathon Man**

"God determines how fast you're going to run; I can only help with the mechanics." **- Bill Bowerman**

"My whole feeling in terms of racing is that you have to be very bold. You sometimes have to be aggressive and gamble." **- Bill Rodgers**

"Second place is not a defeat. It is a stimulation to get better. It makes you even more determined." **- Carlos Lopes**

"Go out hard, when it hurts speed up." **- Matt Carpenter**

"Only those who will risk going too far can possibly find out how far one can go." **- T.S. Eliot**

"Adversity causes some men to break; others to break records." - **William Arthur Ward**

"It's the training that gets you to the starting line. It's the pacing and energy management that gets you to the finish line." - **Kenneth Harkless**

"It is not the mountain we conquer, but ourselves." - **Sir Edmund Hillary**

"More powerful than the will to win is the courage to begin." - **Author Unknown**

"Challenges are what make life interesting; overcoming them is what makes life meaningful." - **Joshua J. Marine**

"It's easier to go down a hill than up it but the view is much better at the top." - **Henry Ward Beecher**

"Most people never run far enough on their first wind to find out they've got a second. Give your dreams all

you've got and you'll be amazed at the energy that comes out of you." - **William James**

"Motivation is what gets you started. Habit is what keeps you going." - **Jim Ryun**

"The most important key to achieving great success is to decide upon your goal and launch, get started, take action, move." - **John Wooden**

"For me, races are the celebration of my training." -- **Dan Browne, 2007 National Champion in the 5K and 20K**

"Do a little more each day than you think you possibly can." -- **Lowell Thomas**

"My feeling is that any day I am too busy to run is a day that I am too busy." - **John Bryant**

"There are clubs you can't belong to, neighborhoods you can't live in, schools you can't get into, but the roads are always open." - **Nike**

"Don't fear moving slowly forward...fear standing still." - **Kathleen Harris**

"Run if you can, walk if you have to, crawl if you must; just never give up." - **Dean Karnazes**

"Your biggest task is not to get ahead of others, but to surpass yourself." - **Author Unknown**

"The obsession with running is really an obsession with the potential for more and more life." - **George Sheehan**

Helpful Resources

Nutrition:

www.smoothiesforrunners.com/vitamix-blender - my favorite blender

www.smoothiesforrunners.com/protein-powder - my favorite protein powder for smoothies

www.smoothiesforrunners.com/iherb - Natural Health products at lower prices

www.getstartedwithjuiceplus.com - the only supplement I promote - whole food based nutrition

Training:

www.trainwellracewell.com – my running blog

www.facebook.com/runningtipsandadvice - our Facebook page...please "like" us!

www.runnersworld.com - articles, race finder, training plans, blogs

www.runningtimes.com - articles, training advice, stories

www.running.competitor.com - articles, stories, nutrition, training advice

www.coolrunning.com - race results, race calendar, training advice www.jeffgalloway.com - expert advice, training plans, resources

www.trailrunnermag.com - trail running articles, trail race finder, stories

www.irunfar.com - for those who aspire to run ultras (anything longer than marathon)

Gear:

www.smoothiesforrunners.com/altrec - outdoor gear, clothing, shoes

www.runnersdepot.org - running gear for runners at any level

Personal Growth:

www.bodyandsoulpublishing.com - more books we've written

A sample from, "**Smoothies For Runners**: *32 Proven Smoothie Recipes to Take Your Running Performance to the Next Level, Decrease Your Recovery Time and Allow You to Run Injury-Free*", also by CJ Hitz

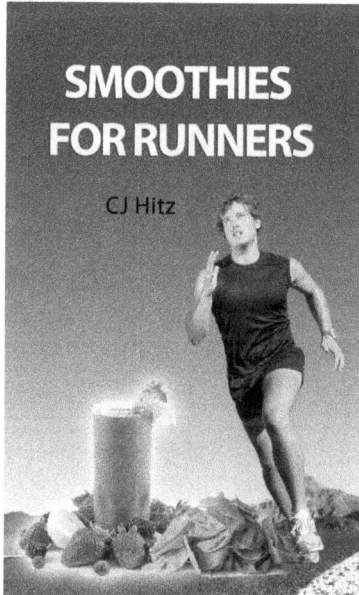

www.SmoothiesForRunners.com

Oatmeal Octane

Some of you may remember those Quaker Oats commercials when Wilford Brimley used to say, "Eat your oatmeal, it's the right thing to do." He was right, of course (I wouldn't argue with him). Oats have a host of benefits including the most popular being the lowering of cholesterol. They're also high in fiber which helps bind up waste and clean the colon. Oats have unique antioxidants called avenanthramides that help prevent free radicals from damaging LDL cholesterol, one of the main causes of cardiovascular disease. Raspberries contain 50% more antioxidant activity than strawberries and also serve to help lower nagging inflammation. This blend is a great fuel choice for that upcoming half-marathon or longer race.

Ingredients
1 cup coconut water
½ cup frozen raspberries
¼ cup plain low fat yogurt or plain *cultured coconut milk yogurt (vegan)
1 frozen ripe banana
½ cup rolled oats
1 Tbs raw honey

Directions
Blend all ingredients until smooth

Recipe Tips
*Cultured coconut milk yogurt is dairy-free and made from coconuts. *"So Delicious"* is one such brand.

Nutrition Facts
Nutrition (per serving): 475 calories, 39 calories from fat, 4.7g total fat, 3.7mg cholesterol, 301.5mg sodium, 1479.5mg potassium, 101.3g carbohydrates, 15.4g fiber, 53.5g sugar, 12.5g protein.

Go to the link below to get 31 more nutritious and delicious smoothies for runners plus more valuable information...
http://www.amazon.com/dp/B0072ZI616

Who is CJ?

CJ Hitz caught the "running bug" in 2008 and has not looked back since. He's dropped nearly forty pounds in weight and continues to see improvement as each year passes. CJ has competed in well over 100 races ranging from road 5Ks to trail 50Ks, including the 17 trail races he ran en route to winning the 2009 *Trail Runner Trophy Series* 30-39 age group and placing 2nd overall.

CJ and his wife Shelley reside in Colorado Springs, CO where they are spoiled beyond measure with running trails and sunshine. They've written several other books which can be found at their website…
www.BodyAndSoulPublishing.com

CJ's personal bests since picking up running again:
*Mile - 5:10 (2011)
*5k - 17:40 (2011)
*4 mile - 23:36 (2011)
*10 mile - 1:00:24 (2011)
*Half-Marathon - 1:22:17 (2011)
*25k - 1:40:59 (2011)

Get more running advice from CJ here:
www.TrainWellRaceWell.com

"Dear friend, I pray that you may enjoy good health and that all may go well with you, even as your soul is getting along well." - 3 John 1:2 (NIV)

Contact

I'd love to hear from you! What did you find most helpful from this book? Or just stop by and say *"hello!"*

Please consider giving me a review on Amazon when you have time.

Connect with me online here:
www.facebook.com/runningtipsandadvice

I look forward to hearing from you!

Here's to many great runs ahead,
CJ

www.ingramcontent.com/pod-product-compliance
Lightning Source LLC
Chambersburg PA
CBHW060333050426
42449CB00011B/2745